D0772426

Someone Special Just Like You

Holt, Rinehart and Winston · New York

Someone Special♡ Just Like You

Text by **Tricia Brown**

Photographs by **Fran Ortiz**

Bibliography by Effie Lee Morris

TO THE CHILDREN

A portion of the royalties from the sales of this book will
be donated to the Easter Seal Infant Development Program.

Copyright © 1982, 1984 by Tricia Brown and Fran Ortiz
Bibliography copyright © 1984 by Effie Lee Morris
All rights reserved, including the right to reproduce this
book or portions thereof in any form.
Published by Holt, Rinehart and Winston,
383 Madison Avenue, New York, New York 10017.
Published simultaneously in Canada by Holt, Rinehart and
Winston of Canada, Limited.

Library of Congress Cataloging in Publication Data
Brown, Tricia.
Someone special, just like you.
Bibliography: p.
1. Handicapped children.   I. Ortiz, Fran.   II. Title.
HV888.B76 1984   362.4′088054   83-18377
ISBN: 0-03-069706-9

First Edition

Designer: Amy Hill
Printed in the United States of America
10 9 8 7 6 5 4 3 2

ISBN 0-03-069706-9

PREFACE

This book began because of a little girl in my son's nursery school class. She had a disability. I wanted to find a book for my own child to help him understand that we should accept one another for the love we have to share with the world, and not judge on the basis of physical appearances or limitations. As I searched for such a book, I learned that none existed.

Fran and I originally intended this book for preschoolers, hoping to help them to accept and to become more comfortable with the children with disabilities they will meet, as these children are increasingly assimilated into the everyday classroom. As we progressed, it became apparent that this was not only a book about children with disabilities, but about all of us. Young and old alike, we all have our own disabilities in one way or another, and each of us is someone special.

Tricia Brown

Meet
someone
special,

someone
just like
you.

Someone
who
may not
walk the
same
way
you do,

9

or hear
the same
sounds,

or see
the same
things.

But just
like you . . .

she likes
to blow
bubbles,

eat
ice cream,

and smell
pretty
flowers.

And,
like you,
she likes to
have fun—

and go
down slides,

play with toys,

and go swimming.

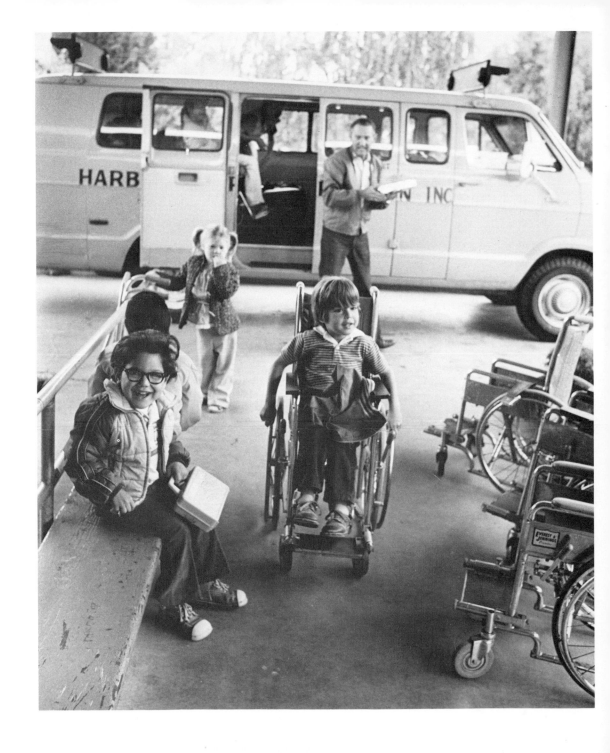

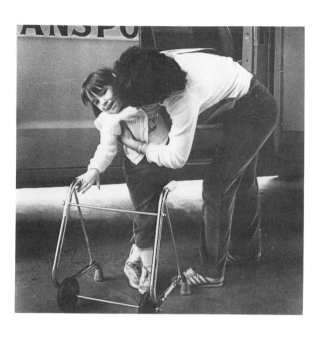

He likes to go
to school,

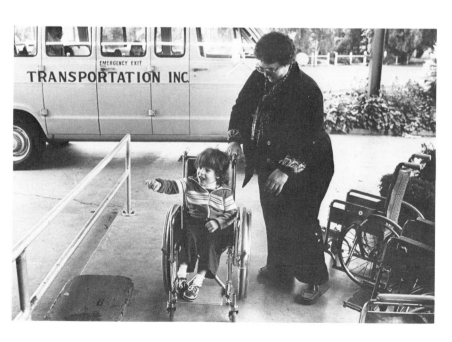

and do art,

and learn from his teacher
how to talk with his hands
if he can't hear,

and read with her fingers
if she can't see.

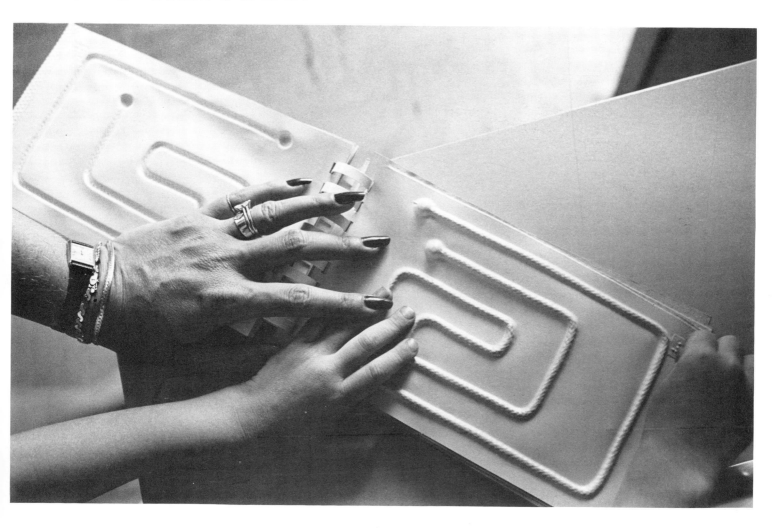

He likes
school trips—

especially to
a science museum

or to the
aquarium!

Then, she
likes to go
home,

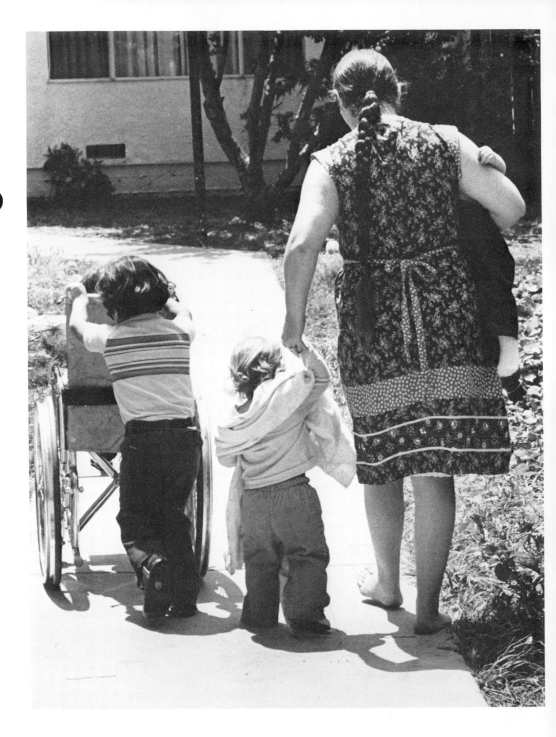

eat lunch,

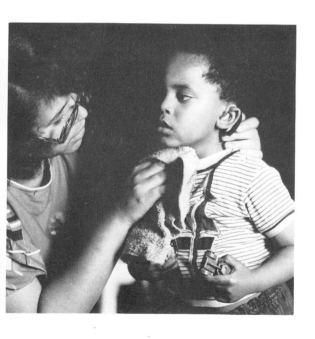

wash up,

and have
quiet time.

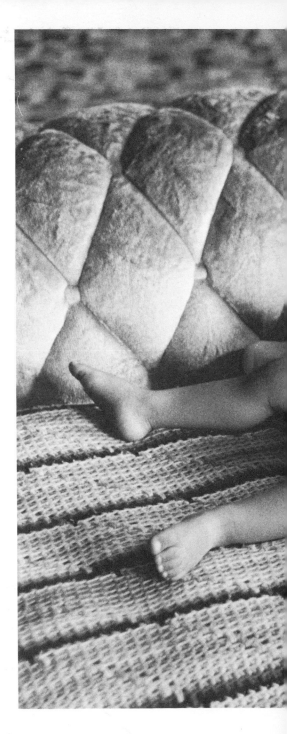

Sometimes, he is lonely—

like times
when he is
waiting for
his dad.

And sometimes he cries when it hurts.

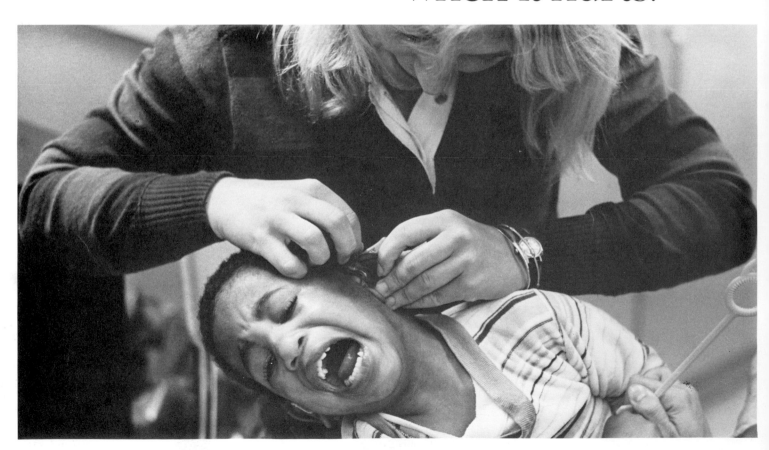

Whenever
he falls
down,
just like
you,
he gets
himself
right
up again.

For
even without seeing
the same things
you do,

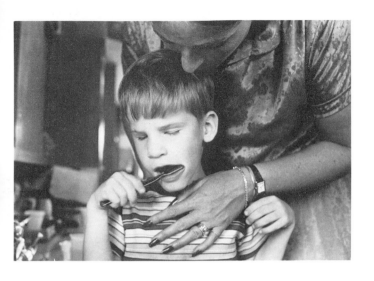

he can
brush
his teeth,

pet
a rabbit,

and walk a
balance beam.

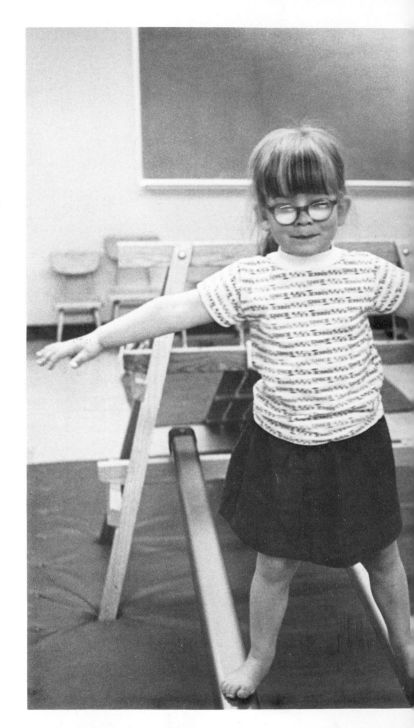

Even without hearing
the same sounds you do,
he can

play
the piano,

talk on the
telephone,

and
listen to
sleepytime
stories.

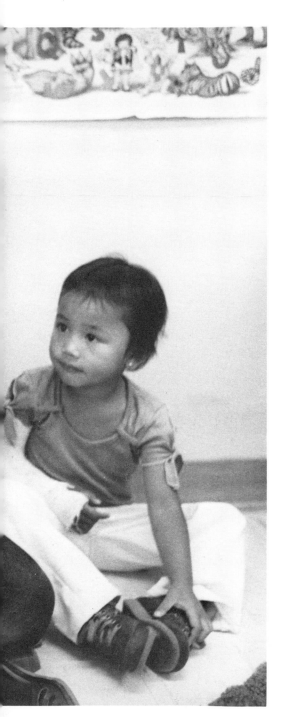

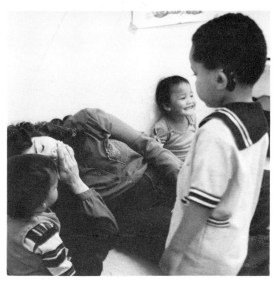

Even without walking
the same way you do,
she can do all the same things
that you like to do:

dance,

swing,

and,
best of
all,
help a
friend.

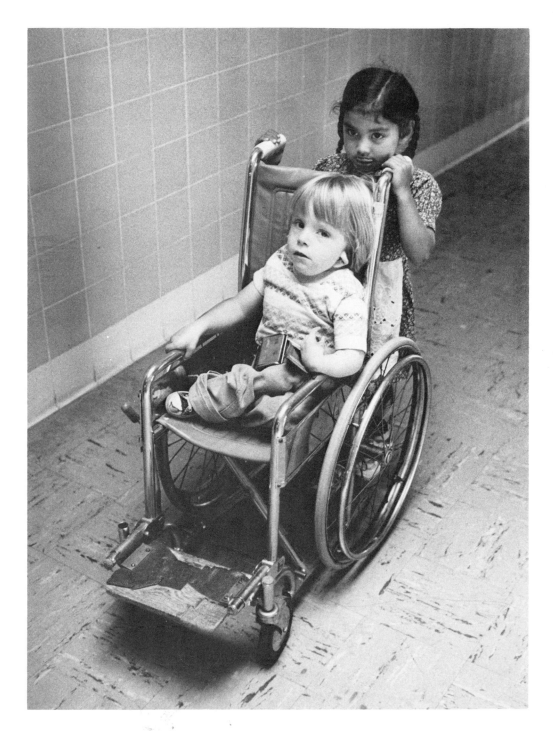

What makes someone special
are the same things
that make you special, too!

A
beautiful
smile,

sweet
kisses,

and lots
of hugs.

BIBLIOGRAPHY

Compiled and annotated by Effie Lee Morris, Lecturer, Children's Literature, Mills College, and former Coordinator, Children's Services, San Francisco Public Library.

ADULT BOOKS

Adams, Barbara, comp. *Like It Is: Facts and Feelings About Handicaps from Kids You Know.* New York: Walker and Co., 1979. A realistic and honest presentation by handicapped children who tell in their own way about their various handicaps, their special needs, and their desires to be treated like everyone else.

Blank, Joseph P. *19 Steps up the Mountain: The Story of the DeBolt Family.* Philadelphia: J. B. Lippincott, 1976. The inspiring story of Robert and Dorothy DeBolt and his, her, and their adopted "hard to place" children with handicaps. The DeBolts are the founders of AASK (Aid to Adoption of Special Kids).

Buscaglia, Leo. *The Disabled and Their Parents: A Counseling Challenge.* Rev. ed. New York: Holt, Rinehart and Winston, 1983. Leo Buscaglia believes that disabled individuals and their families are "in desperate need of reality-based guidance." He challenges the helping professionals to provide better information on the nature and implications of each disability and the complex problems of day-to-day living. The consumers of these services will be enlightened by his forthrightness.

Butler, Dorothy. *Cushla and Her Books.* Boston: Horn Book, 1980. Cushla, born with multiple physical handicaps, developed slowly, requiring constant care. Her young parents read aloud to her to pass the time, and their reading made significant changes in her early development. This is an inspiring testimonial to books and reading and their effect on the life of a child.

Doyle, Phyllis B., John F. Goodman, Jeffrey M. Grotsky, and Lester Mann. *Helping the Severely Handicapped Child: A Guide for Parents and Teachers.* Illustrated by Joseph E. Connolly. New York: Thomas Y. Crowell, 1979. In simple, straightforward language, the book answers questions on public school training, how to help the child at home, where to find help—e.g., services, camps, special equipment—and concludes with information on placement and educational problems of the child in public school. Bibliography included.

Featherstone, Helen. *A Difference in the Family: Life with a Disabled Child.* New York: Basic Books, 1980. The mother of a disabled child writes of her personal experiences as well as those of others in families with a special child. She tells how a child's handicap touches the lives of those around him or her and often provides comfort and reassurance to relatives, friends, and professionals. A sincere and readable book.

Feingold, S. Norman, and Norman Miller. *Your Future: A Guide for the Handicapped Teenager.* Rev. ed. New York: Richards Rosen Press, 1982. Many adolescents with disabilities plan to live independent lives. Here, opportunities and obstacles facing the handicapped are carefully evaluated for these teenagers.

Gliedman, John, and William Roth. *The Unexpected Minority: Handicapped Children in America.* For The Carnegie Council on Children. New York: Harcourt

Brace Jovanovich, 1980. An important, well-written volume on the results of research about disabled children in America.

Greenfeld, Josh. *A Child Called Noah*. New York: Holt, Rinehart and Winston, 1972.

———*A Place for Noah*. New York: Holt, Rinehart and Winston, 1978. A father writes a frank and passionate account of bringing up a brain-damaged son. The all-consuming, complex, and devastating problems the family faces are met with courage, spirit, and love.

Kamien, Janet. *What If You Couldn't . . . ? A Book about Special Needs*. Illustrated by Signe Henson. New York: Charles Scribner's Sons, 1979. Clear explanations of six handicaps—blindness, deafness, dyslexia, emotional problems, impaired mobility, and mental retardation—are given to dispel ignorance and hostility. The author not only asks the reader to imagine having a disability, but also provides experiments that will help the reader to understand how it actually feels.

Larrick, Nancy. *A Parent's Guide to Children's Reading*. 5th ed. New York: Bantam Books, 1982. With illustrations from favorite children's books. This well-known, useful book, now in its fifth edition, gives anecdotes about books and reading as well as advice and a bibliography of recommended books to share with children.

Mitchell, Joyce Slayton. *Taking on the World: Empowering Strategies for Parents of Children with Disabilities*. New York: Harcourt Brace Jovanovich, 1982. An enthusiastic, action-filled manual with step-by-step directions and practical advice on how to be an advocate for children with disabilities.

Stein, Sarah Bennett. *About Handicaps: An Open Family Book for Parents and Children Together*. Photographs by Dick Frank. New York: Walker and Co., 1974. Two books in one: a story for children is accompanied by an interpretive text for adults which runs alongside. In the children's story, Matthew fears and mocks Joe, who has cerebral palsy. His understanding father introduces him to Mr. Bello, a veteran with an artificial arm. Mr. Bello explains to Matthew how the arm works and then tells the boy about his concern that people would no longer like him after he lost his arm. Matthew and his father discuss his fears and ignorance. Slowly Matthew learns to accept Joe. An effective and moving book with sensitive photographs.

Sullivan, Mary Beth, Alan J. Brightman, and Joseph Blatt; with Margaret Roberts and JoAnn Williams Fiske. *Feeling Free*. Illustrated by Marci Davis and Linda Bourke; photographs by Alan J. Brightman. Reading, Mass.: Addison-Wesley, 1979. Candid statements from children with five handicaps—deafness, blindness, learning disabilities, dwarfism, and cerebral palsy—help dispel the myths and stereotypes surrounding those disabilities. Included are interviews, cartoons, games, puzzles, and stories. The book is based on a television series of the same title.

CHILDREN'S BOOKS
Preschool through ages 5 to 8

General

Buscaglia, Leo. *Because I Am Human*. Photographs by Bruce Ferguson. Thorofare, N.J.: Charles B. Slack, 1972. "Because I am human there are so many wonderful things I can do. . . . I can smell a flower. . . . I can hug. . . . I can go to sleep when I am tired. . . . I can think happy thoughts. . . . I can love. . . ." The feeling for the joy of life builds through the expressive text and sensitive photographs of children and adults. A book to be shared.

Hearing-Impaired

Arthur, Catherine. *My Sister's Silent World*. Pictures by Nathan Talbot. Chicago: Children's Press, 1979. Little sister describes her adored big sister's hearing problem and tells of a happy family visit to the zoo.

Bourke, Linda. *Handmade ABC: A Manual Alphabet.* Illustrated by the author. Reading, Mass.: Addison-Wesley, 1981. In simple black-and-white sketches, each letter of the alphabet is shown and illustrated by its own handshape. This beginning interpretation of finger spelling can encourage anyone to try the technique.

Charlip, Remy, Mary Beth Charlip, and George Ancona. *Handtalk: An ABC of Finger Spelling and Sign Language.* Photographs. New York: Parents Magazine Press, 1974. In large color photographs, expressive models use hands, faces, and bodies to interpret a letter of the alphabet in sign language. The letter and its finger sign are shown in the corner of the page. Some words beginning with the letter are spelled out in sign across the bottom. In addition, the entire alphabet in finger spelling appears in black-and-white photographs on the first two pages. This was the first book for children to introduce the two kinds of sign language—finger spelling and signing. Although the book's entire effect is somewhat overwhelming, its value lies in the broad overview of the techniques and in showing that being deaf is no deterrent to a joyous and happy existence.

Montgomery, Elizabeth Rider. *The Mystery of the Boy Next Door.* Illustrated by Ethel Gold. Champaign, Ill.: Garrard Publishing Co., 1978. When the neighborhood children discover that the boy next door is deaf, they understand why he seemed unfriendly. Their attitudes change when they discover that he can talk with his hands. A chart of the alphabet in sign language is included.

Peter, Diana. *Claire and Emma.* Photographs by Jeremy Finlay. New York: Harper and Row, John Day, 1977. The mother of four-year-old Claire and two-year-old Emma describes their hearing aids and their lessons in lipreading and lipspeaking. The sisters, who were born deaf, are lively and enjoy the same things that other children do. The emphasis is on the special communication skills needed by two little girls who have normal intelligence, abilities, and interests.

Peterson, Jeanne Whitehouse. *I Have a Sister. My Sister Is Deaf.* Illustrated by Deborah Ray. New York: Harper and Row, 1977. Two sisters play together doing all the things a young deaf girl can do when lovingly supported by her sensitive older sister. Her accomplishments and strengths as well as the compensations she must make are described. The poetic text and appropriate illustrations make this book particularly appealing to young children who are deaf or who have a relationship with someone who has this handicap.

Sullivan, Mary Beth, and Linda Bourke; with Susan Regan. *A Show of Hands.* Illustrated by Linda Bourke. Reading, Mass.: Addison-Wesley, 1980. A lighthearted, clever presentation of the way hands are used in communication. Everyone uses hands to send messages. The cartoon-like illustrations and brief text remind readers that the use of hands is natural. Finger spelling and methods of attracting the attention of the deaf are included among the various ways of communication.

Wolf, Bernard. *Anna's Silent World.* Photographs by the author. New York: Harper and Row, 1977. Family support, special training, and technology help Anna, a six-year-old girl who was born deaf, to participate in normal activities. In this photo-documentary, her deafness is explained; and lipreading, her hearing aid, and other forms of therapy are described. A warm and sensitive story of a family living with a disabled child.

Mentally Handicapped

Brightman, Alan. *Like Me.* Photographs. Boston: Little, Brown and Co., 1976. Photographs in color and a simple lyrical text show and tell about mentally handicapped children playing and interacting with others. The emphasis is on the children's similarities rather than on their differences.

Clifton, Lucille. *My Friend Jacob.* Illustrated by Thomas DiGrazia. New York: E. P. Dutton, 1980. Sam tells the story of his best friend Jacob, who is older and stronger and taller but who "forgets." They help each other with their respective skills and Sam claims victory when he helps Jacob to learn to knock before he opens a door. The friendship between the two boys can provide a happy example for other children.

Larsen, Hanne. *Don't Forget Tom.* Photographs by the author. New York: Thomas Y. Crowell, 1978. Tom is six years old and mentally handicapped. Some things are harder for him than for other children his age. The things he and his family do together are reported with empathy and photographed in color with skill.

Lasker, Joe. *He's My Brother.* Illustrated by the author. Niles, Ill.: Albert Whitman, 1974. A loving older brother explains how Jamie copes with his mental handicap and the difficulties he encounters in the family and with his peers.

Smith, Lucia B. *A Special Kind of Sister.* Illustrated by Chuck Hall. New York: Holt, Rinehart and Winston, 1979. Seven-year-old Sarah's older brother is mentally handicapped. Sarah struggles with her feelings about Andy and her feelings about herself. A good picture of retardation and its effect on the family from a young child's perspective.

Sobol, Harriet. *My Brother Steven Is Retarded.* Photographs by Patricia Agre. New York: Macmillan Co., 1977. Beth is eleven with an older mentally retarded brother. She loves him, but sometimes he embarrasses her and makes her angry. Through her own feelings, she explains what it is like to be part of a family in which one person is retarded. Photographs show positive family life.

Physically Disabled

Fanshawe, Elizabeth. *Rachel.* Illustrated by Michael Charlton. Scarsdale, N.Y.: Bradbury Press, 1975. Rachel enjoys life. She has fun as she participates in many activities at home, at school, and on vacation—in her wheelchair. A good explanation of the similarities and differences of disabled people that young children can understand.

Fassler, Joan. *Howie Helps Himself.* Illustrated by Joe Lasker. Niles, Ill.: Albert Whitman, 1975. Howie must be confined to a wheelchair because he has cerebral palsy. He wants very much to move his wheelchair by himself. He tries and tries and at last succeeds in racing happily across the room to his proud waiting father. Howie sets a goal, accomplishes it, and is thrilled by his success, just as any child would be. A solid and satisfactory story. Further information available from NACAC, 3900 Market St., Suite 247, Riverside, CA 92501.

Mack, Nancy. *Tracy.* Photographs by Heinz Kluetmeier. Milwaukee: Raintree Publishers, 1976. Tracy has cerebral palsy. The photographs show her at school and at therapy sessions in a wheelchair or on crutches. Tracy sets limited goals, achieves them, and is rewarded by the teasing of classmates—the final sign of acceptance. A successful story of mainstreaming.

Menotti, Gian-Carlo. *Amahl and the Night Visitors.* Narrative adaptation by Frances Frost. Illustrated by Roger Duvoisin. New York: McGraw-Hill, 1972. Amahl, the little lame shepherd boy, entertained the Wise Men on their way to Bethlehem. They took his simple gift to the Christ Child, and Amahl received a miraculous gift in return. The opera is often performed during the holiday season for children, who understand and accept the miracle. In this adaptation, the exact dialogue of the opera is preserved.

Rabe, Berniece. *The Balancing Girl.* Pictures by Lillian Hoban. New York: E. P. Dutton, 1981. Margaret balances well in her wheelchair and on her crutches. She balances magic markers and cans for the teachers, too. When she balances dominoes for the school carnival, everyone sees her skill.

Tate, Joan. *Ben and Annie.* Illustrated by Judith Gwyn Brown. New York: Doubleday and Co., 1974. Annie is delighted when Ben gives her wheelchair rides down the hill, but a misinterpretation by a well-meaning adult puts an end to the happy excursion. Children will understand the game and its potential for danger, yet their sympathies will be for Ben and Annie in this realistic story.

White, Paul. *Janet at School.* Illustrated by Jeremy Finlay. New York: Thomas Y. Crowell, 1978. Five-year-old Janet was born with *spina bifida.* Unable to use her legs, she must use a wheelchair. Janet, her family, and friends learn to cope with her problems so that she can be involved in many activities. A simple smooth text, which includes an explanation of the handicap, and excellent color photographs provide a positive and engaging account of a cheerful little girl.

Wolf, Bernard. *Don't Feel Sorry for Paul.* Photographs by author. Philadelphia: J. B. Lippincott Co., 1974. (Spanish edition available. *No sientan lástima por Paul.* Edited by Victoria Ortiz. Translated by Ximena Lois. Philadelphia: Libros Lippincott en Español, 1977.) Paul has adjusted to the artificial limbs that replace the incomplete hands and feet with which he was born. Factual information about prosthetic devices and a visit to the Institute of Rehabilitative Medicine are shown in accompanying photographs.

Visually Disabled

Goodsell, Jane. *Katie's Magic Glasses.* Illustrated by Barbara Cooney. Boston: Houghton Mifflin Co., 1965. An amusing rhyming story of five-year-old Katie's experiences—needing glasses, experimenting with her father's, and finally joyously seeing the world through her very own pair.

Jensen, Virginia Allen, and Polly Edman. *Red Thread Riddles.* New York: Philomel Books, 1980. Follow the raised red thread by sight and touch to the riddle questions. See and feel the raised pictures of the everyday objects. Read the answers in print and Braille. A "together" experience for blind and sighted friends.

Jensen, Virginia Allen, and Woodbury Haller. *What's That?* New York: Philomel Books, 1978. In the print story, four little friends are looking for Little Shaggy, who is wanted at home. The characters are illustrated by shapes made of various textures to be felt as the story is read aloud. Little Shaggy is found and the story comes to a satisfactory conclusion for fingers and ears. Award for graphic excellence at the International Children's Book Fair, Bologna, 1978.

Keats, Ezra Jack. *Apartment Three.* Illustrated by the author. New York: Macmillan Co., 1971. Two young brothers hear someone in their apartment building playing a harmonica. Searching for the source of the music, Sam and Ben find a lonely blind man, whom they approach with apprehension and fear. The man astonishes them with what he has learned about the world through his hearing and with what he can say about it through his music. A positive introduction to blind adults for children, as ignorance and rejection are supplanted by information and friendship.

MacLachlen, Patricia. *Through Grandpa's Eyes.* Illustrated by Deborah Ray. New York: Harper and Row, 1980. John's loving and caring grandfather is blind. He teaches John, who can see, a different way of seeing with fingers, ears, and heart.

Newth, Philip. *Roly Goes Exploring.* Translated from the Swedish by the author. New York: Philomel Books, 1981. Illustrations cut out of cardboard encourage awareness of geometric shapes and patterns through visual and tactile experiences. Simple text about Roly, a small, round, curious circle, has added dimension with Braille and print side-by-side on the page. Best of all, blind, visually handicapped, and sighted children can read and enjoy together.

Raskin, Ellen. *Spectacles.* Illustrated by the author. New York: Atheneum, 1969. Irrepressible Iris, a delightful heroine, needs glasses, but she resists wearing them. Only when she discovers their glamorous potential does she consent. Witty illustrations add to the entertaining text.

Sargent, Susan, and Donna Aaron West. *My Favorite Place*. Illustrated by Allen Eitzen. Nashville: Abingdon Press, 1983. In a visit to the seashore, a blind child discovers the importance of the other four senses.

Yolen, Jane. *The Seeing Stick*. Illustrated by Remy Charlip and Demetra Maraslis. New York: Thomas Y. Crowell, 1977.
The emperor promises a fortune to anyone who can help his beloved princess, Hwei Ming, to see. A strange old man claims his "seeing stick" will cure her. He helps her "to grow eyes at the tips of her fingers" and, more important, to see with her mind and her heart. When the princess learns the old man's surprising secret, she more deeply appreciates the miracles of his lessons. The ancient human problems are sensitively re-created in a modern literary folktale.

ACKNOWLEDGMENTS

The author and photographer gratefully acknowledge the following teachers, administrators, parents and consultants whose enthusiasm, cooperation and support made this book possible: Karen Rassi, Jay Katz, Recreation Center for the Handicapped, San Francisco; Sandy Cantando, Project Idea/Visually Impaired Preschool, Coventry School, Campbell, California; Mary Molacavage, Robin Ludmer, Jill Boxerman, Center for the Education of the Infant Deaf, San Francisco; Ellen Schnur, Martin Gabriel, Sunset School, Physically Handicapped Unit, San Lorenzo Unified School District, California; Barbara McKeag, Paula Minkus, Carrie Manuel, Lucy Stofle-Anderson, Telegraph Hill Nursery School, San Francisco; Pacific Primary School, San Francisco; Pat Azarnoff, Pediatric Projects, Inc., Santa Monica, California; Dr. and Mrs. Gerald Clum, Mr. and Mrs. David Falcon, Mr. and Mrs. Leonard Medina, Mr. and Mrs. Robert Blackstone, Mr. and Mrs. Robert Caloroso, Mr. and Mrs. Larry Cotton, Roberta Reyes, Barbara Smith, Sharon Cameron, Eddie Dyba, Robert Conover, Beth Tufts, Tom Tufts, Jim Jackman, Judy Karasik, Marjorie Creazzi, Catherine Ortiz, Theodore Brown, and Barrett Brown.

Our deepest debt is owed to the children we photographed whose joy welcomed us into their hearts: Chris Blackstone, Kate Bristow, Adam Brotherton, Bridget Caloroso, Cassie Clum, Scooter Cotton, Barrett Dull, Jimmy Falcon, Michael Ghersetti, Miranda Green, Jonathan Hacker, Laura Hays, Maggie Medina, Joseph Mesa, Jr., Erika Miller, Robert Morales, Tory Neubert, Shaun Reynolds, Sukhraj Sandu, Barbara Smith, David Stewart, Elsa Vallejo, Jason Woo, and Jonathan Woo.